WHY ISRAEL IS WINNING THE BATTLES BUT LOSING THE WAR

BY

S. Mugwa Tebid

Introduction

In 1947, when the United Nations met to decide on the creation of the Jewish state of Israel, 33 member states voted in favor of, 13 mostly Arab states voted against, and only 10 abstained.

In 2011, when UNESCO met to decide on the admission of the Palestinian Authority, 107 members voted against the Israeli position, with only 14 members voting with Israel.

In 2012, when the United Nations General Assembly met to elevate the Palestinian Authority to observer status, 138 members voted against the Israeli position and only 8 voted with Israel.

Since its creation at the end of the Second World War, the state of Israel has turned out to be the most successful new state in human history. Its contributions in science and technology to the well-being of humanity, relative to its size, are unparalleled. The trials and tribulations it has endured and survived since 1948 have been herculean.

Yet, rather than an embrace and celebration of this success, there appears to be an increasing isolation of the Jewish state in the international community, while its vile enemies gain more and more acceptance.

It would appear that the international community has developed an extremely short memory and that the frequency of genocidal wars during the last few decades has numbed consciences to the extent that we have all forgotten the cruel persecutions visited upon the Jewish people throughout their history and more recently, by the Nazis and the Stalinists, partially the impetus for the creation of the Jewish state of Israel.

The growing hostility towards Israel would of itself be a human tragedy. But this is further compounded by an increasing number of countries governed by terrorist organizations and states committed to the destruction of Israel and the annihilation of Jews. When an organization such as UNESCO embraces groups that preach racial hatred and religious intolerance, and co-sponsors schools that teach hatreds of all kinds, it is time for the international community to wake up.

When the United Nations allows some of its members to threaten another member with genocide and annihilation, a complete negation of its charter, all people of goodwill have to rise up and ask for answers.

The Prime Minister of Israel, Benjamin Netanyahu, has been criticized for his blunt, undiplomatic style in his interactions with other foreign leaders. These critics have sought to attribute the growing isolation of Israel to the efforts of a leader who, like a voice in the wilderness, is trying to draw the attention of a drowsy world to the developing threats to Israel and the civilized world from medieval religious fundamentalists. Other critics have attributed the isolation to an ineffective and ineffectual Israeli diplomatic service that serves the country very poorly, depriving its people of the many friends they so rightly deserve. Yet other people have pointed to ineffective pro-Israel lobbying groups in America who, while successful in buying and bullying political leaders, are actually alienating an increasing number of ordinary citizens.

Valid or not, these criticisms cannot account for the increasing anti-Israel feelings within the international community at large. The belief here is that there are many other contributing factors, most of which are beyond the power and influence of the Israeli government and its citizens.

When votes are traded at the UN and UNESCO like stocks on the New York Stock Exchange, no one can blame Israel for the moral turpitude of the member states. Prior to the aforementioned 2011 UNESCO vote and the 2012 UN vote, agents from some Gulf states made generous donations to officials from at least five African countries: two from West Africa and three from Central and Southern Africa.

Another prominent foot soldier in the war against the state of Israel has been the liberal European and North American press. No other country in the world is subjected to the wrongful vilification visited daily upon Israel by the world press, particularly the western media. Aggressive terrorist organizations such as Hamas and Hezbollah are portrayed as victims, while Israelis fighting in self-defense are labeled aggressors. The western press has been known to fudge events, complete with fake pictures, just to vilify Israel and turn international public opinion against it.

In matters pertaining to the Middle East, with the rare exception of the Fox News Corporation, the western press has abdicated its role as agents of information and education to become agents of disinformation and propaganda for Israel's enemies.

One cannot truthfully examine Israel's declining diplomatic fortunes without looking at the role of the age-old disease of anti-Semitism. During the past two decades, the world has witnessed a renaissance of anti-Semitism in a form as vicious as that of the Weimar Republic and later, Nazi Germany. This new anti-Semitism started as an infection of disaffected skinheads and the like but has now spread to otherwise respectable company.

Many world leaders today, in business as well as politics, openly spew their anti-Semitism without fear of stigma or reprisal. Iranian president Mahmoud Ahmadinejad is regularly given the UN podium for his anti-Semitic rants. It is becoming more acceptable for leading party and elected officials in Europe to not only announce their anti-Semitism but also espouse and hail acts of violence against Jews. Over the past decade, the world has, without any reaction, watched the rate of acts of violence against Jews and Jewish institutions in Europe and North America increase annually by at least 30%.

The government of Israel has no control over the increasing tolerance of anti-Semitism. Neither can it, as a functioning democracy, control the unbridled infamy of CNN, the BBC, etc. It is the responsibility of the civilized to call them out for what they are.

Israel, the primary victim of Islamic fundamentalism, is being blamed for the spreading of this cancer and the terrorism that is attendant to it. Those casting blame, however, fail to acknowledge the motivations and goals of the mullahs of Tehran, who are the world's principal sponsors of Islamic terrorism. It is this naïveté vis-à-vis Iranian motivations that predicate the erroneous belief that a peace treaty between Israel and the Palestinians will resolve the problems of Islamic terrorism.

The mullahs and ayatollahs of Iran do not care about the Palestinians' fate. Their dog in the hunt is the created of a world caliphate under Iranian leadership. Since the days of Darius I, Iranians have considered Arabs a primitive people and think they are undeserving of the custodianship of the Islamic holy cities of Mecca and Medina.

Iranian leaders consider Israel the only formidable obstacle in the region to the realization of their caliphate. Their crusade against Israel will only end when the state of Israel is annihilated, including its Arab citizens, many of whom are Christian.

Contrary to what western anti-Semites may believe, the subways of Paris, London, and New York are not threatened by Israel or Jewish fanatics but rather by the agents of intolerance sponsored by Middle Eastern monarchs and ayatollahs. When airline passengers are stripped, searched, and humiliated at airports around the world, it is not out of fear of some Jewish conspiracy. It is because of a fatwa from some desert-dwelling mullah from Qom.

Today, the hatred of Jews may be the motivating force that drives the Iranian pursuit of nuclear weapons but tomorrow, when the nuclear cloud settles over cities or oceans, it will be the whole world that mourns. Nazism did not just kill Jews. Their folly cost the world more than 32 million other lives. Bad things only happen when good people stay silent. Must we repeat the errors of the past?

CHAPTER ONE: The Renaissance of Anti-Semitism

Too many overly enthusiastic supporters of the state of Israel equate any criticism of the Israeli government with anti-Semitism. If that were true, most Israeli citizens would qualify as anti-Semites. Israel, the only real and vibrant democracy in the Middle East, has not had a government in half a century that was no opposed and criticized by roughly half its population.

The truth is, even paranoids have real enemies and Israel, Jews, and Judaism have always had legions of them. Even though Christianity is considered the father of modern anti-Semitism, hatred of Jews and Judaism is as old as monotheism. The persecution of Jews precedes the exodus from Egypt and even the destruction of the Temple of YHW at Elephantine.

The strategic location of Palestine as a trade gateway between Europe and Asia attracted invaders from east and west throughout recorded history. The Romans, Greeks, Babylonians, Persians, and others took turns in the conquest and colonization of Palestine. Each conquest resulted in both the enslavement and exile of the local Jewish population.

In a primitive world ruled by polytheistic kings, the monotheistic Jews' religious practices earned them repeated persecutions, involving forced conversions and, quite often, mass murders. Although we are more familiar today with the genocides of the Spanish Inquisition and those perpetrated by the Nazis and Stalinists, pogroms have been carried out against Jews for thousands of years.

At the end of World War II, the graphic details of the Nazi concentration camps and the general atrocities committed against Jews finally touched the conscience of the civilized world to put an end to the repeated wars on Jews and Judaism.

UN Resolution 181 of 1947 and the subsequent creation of the Jewish state of Israel was a commitment by the international community to offer the Jewish nation a space where they could practice or not practice their faith without the risk of intimidation or oppression. This space happened to be located on their ancestral land.

The commitment of the human community to Jews and Judaism was not just limited to the creation of the state of Israel. It also included the obligation of public education about the danger of all forms of racism, with particular emphasis on anti-Semitism, which has been the most destructive in human history. For a while, the shame of the brutality and cruelty appeared to have been seared in the universal mind. Anti-Semitism saw a rapid decline and the most unrepentant anti-Semites went into the closet.

As the memories of Nazi Germany fade, the world is witnessing a global renaissance of anti-Semitism. Starting in the 1960s as a fad among the disenfranchised, it is now gaining respectability in the media and within normal political circles around the globe. The modern anti-Semite's obvious object of hatred and vilification is Israel.

The attention of the general public is gripped by the rantings of the lunatics in Tehran, thereby often missing the equally insidious anti-Semitic buffoonery of western racists. In 2011, the Southern Poverty Law Center put the number of hate groups in the United States of America at 1018, most of which are anti-Semitic and receive generous financing from a pair of Florida-based billionaires.

In Europe, leading political figures, in some cases members of ruling coalitions, openly flaunt their anti-Semitism without fear of retribution from an electorate that generally shares their prejudices. The most notorious that need special mention here include Nikolao Michaloliakos, found of the Greek party Golden Dawn, and Marton Gyongyosi, a leading member of a right-wing Hungarian political party.

These outspoken leaders are just a manifestation of their societies and their new socio-cultural trends. In 2012, criminal anti-Semitic acts in France increased by 58% (a conservative estimate). In Belgium, the Service for the Protection of the Jewish Community, a government agency, declared criminal anti-Semitic acts had increased by 30%. All the other member states of the European Union have noticed similar, and in some cases higher, rates of crimes against Jews and Jewish institutions within their borders. These crimes include deadly attacks on Jews, destruction of Jewish property and places of worship, and even the desecration of Jewish burial grounds.

This anti-Semitism in Europe seems to have permeated the ruling political class, who has no problem criticizing Israeli leaders and blaming them for all the ills of the world. Their votes in favor of terrorist organizations at the UN and UNESCO is their way of thumbing their noses at the state and people of Israel, even as their constituents and cities live under an existential threat from Arab terrorists and their allies.

The other group that has joined the anti-Israel cabal is so-called liberals and progressives. Half a century ago, liberalism or progressivism was characterized by an ability to question orthodoxy and subject decision-making to analytical and critical thought.

Progressivism today has become just another fad by which liberal intellectuals, dominant in the news media and academia, too lazy to do rigorous research and analysis, spew their prejudices in long-winded and convoluted verbiage. They categorize some people or causes as victims and underdogs, then develop a blind spot in their unalloyed support and advocacy for their protégées.

Concerning the Middle East, western liberals have classified Israel as the bully and villain. Their declared underdogs, i.e. the Arabs, are thus free to carry out any conduct without risk of criticism or loss of support from the western media. Israel gets the blame for anything untowards that happens in the region.

Let us examine some of the accusations of western liberals against Israel. Despite liberals considering Israel a bully, it is public knowledge that the Israeli-Palestinian conflict is the result of the rejection of 1947's UN Resolution 181, mandating the creation of a Jewish state and an Arab state.

When the Jewish state was subsequently formed in 1948, with a population of less than two million, it was attacked by the collective armies of the Arab League. The total population of the Arab League at the time was more than two hundred million; combined, their armies totaled more than the entire population of Israel. The new state of Israel had no time to constitute a standing army, whereas the Arab armies were heavily armed and subsidized by the Soviet Union.

The 1956 war was started by Egypt, which, in breach of the Constantinople Convention of 1888, seized the Suez Canal and blocked the Straits of Tiran and the Gulf of Aqaba.

In 1967, the Egyptians, once again in contravention of international agreements, expelled United Nations Observer forces from the Sinai and crossed UN lines.

In 1973, the Yom Kippur War was the result of an organized assault on Israel by Egypt and Syria, supported by the Arab League. The combined Arab armies that attacked Israel included one million troops, seven hundred aircraft, and three thousand tanks. Israel had less than 400,000 troops, 1700 tanks, and 440 aircraft.

Looking at the facts above, how can anyone with a functioning brain declare Israel the bully and aggressor in the Middle Eastern crisis?

The second accusation liberals make against Israel has to do with the Palestinian refugee problem. Israel is accused of causing this problem and rejecting Palestinians' right of return, which they claim is the greatest impediment to peace in the region.

It is a blatant historical misrepresentation to assign the Palestinian diaspora to Israel. The primary cause of the exile of both Jews and Arabs from Palestine was the numerous conquerors of the region. Another major cause was the inhospitable weather and lack of natural resources for the shepherds who populated the area.

In more recent times, starting with the creation of the state of Israel in 1948, the Arab League ordered all Palestinians to leave the region to make room for the invading armies to easily wipe out the Jewish population before the return of the Palestinians. In 1970, the war between the Jordanian army and the Palestinians led to the exile of some 300,000 refugees.

Most liberals do not seem to have read Resolution 181, which clearly called for the creation of two distinct states: one for Jews and one for Arabs. Israel has already absorbed more than two million Arabs. Why should they be required to absorb more Arabs, which could, in the end, defeat the purpose of having a Jewish state in Palestine? Texas, Arizona, and California were Mexican territories at one time. I have not heard an American liberal advocating for the right of return to all Mexicans. Neither will it be thinkable for a French progressive to advocate for the right of return for Germans to the Alsace and Lorraine regions of France.

Liberals deliberately will not see the responsibility of Palestinian leaders in the plight of their people. The Palestinian Authority receives more than $5 billion in foreign aid every year, and has nothing to show for it. Its revolutionary leaders are busy building personal fortunes, while their families are shopping on the most expensive boulevards in Paris, London, and New York. Yasser Arafat left a personal fortune of nearly $2 billion, even though he never owned so much as a candy store.

The real story behind Palestinians suffering in refugee camps devolves from a deliberate policy by Palestinian leaders to maintain a huge reservoir of very desperate people from which it can recruit suicide bombers. The filthy refugee camps also serve as a good fund-raising tool and propaganda.

Liberals and so-called progressives accuse Israel of being an impediment to peace. Israeli intransigence is said to be the only obstacle to peace in the region. They question the motives of Israeli leaders and accept all Palestinian claims at face value. The question any sensible person should ask is, Who has more of an interest in a peace settlement, the welfare queens of the dictatorial Palestinian leadership or the democratic Israeli government with a prosperous economy? The benefits to Israel of a resolution of the Israeli-Palestinian conflict cannot be overemphasized. Among the many will be reduced military spending and access to a large Middle Eastern market in need of Israeli technology and knowhow.

Western liberals like to forget that in July 2000, President Clinton hosted Prime Minister Ehud Barak and Chairman Arafat at Camp David. The Israeli government offered the Palestinians 97% of the West Bank, the entire Gaza Strip, and other land to compensate for Jewish settlements in the West Bank. Israel was actually offering the Palestinian leader land that was undisputed Israeli territory.

Arafat rejected an offer that was superior to demands he had made on previous occasions. The reason for the rejection was pressure from leaders of his Fatah movement who were afraid of losing much of the financial aid they received from Arab monarchies in the Gulf region. They were not ready to take the responsibility attendant to an independent state and lose Israel as a scapegoat for their failures.

The arrival of Netanyahu has been of great joy to western liberals because his brusque manners are an easy target for attacks. The stall in the peace process has been attributed to his reported stubbornness. But none of his critics have been able to point to the person he should be negotiating with.

Palestinians are hopelessly divided between Fatah and Hamas. Mahmoud Abass, the titular head of the Palestinian Authority, leads a movement that only controls the West Bank. He is not allowed in Gaza, where he has no authority, and is not able to make any agreements that will be binding on Hamas. Hamas controls Gaza but refuses to acknowledge the legitimacy of Israel.

Attempts to initiate Israeli-Palestinian negotiations at this point will simply amount to the perpetuation of a fraud against both the Israeli and Palestinian people, as well as against the international community, because there is no viable Palestinian partner to negotiate with.

Criticism of Israel and its leaders is predicated on the false assumption that Palestinian leaders are actually interested in a final resolution of their conflict with Israel. As previously stated, Arafat's Fatah heirs are not ready to let go of the 'golden goose' that conflict with Israel has been for their personal purses. As for the more radical and less corrupt Hamas, they are drinking the Kool-Aid from Tehran and believing in the chimera of the destruction of Israel by an Iranian nuclear bomb.

European leaders and bankers humor them because most of what Palestinians gather from the Gulf states, United States, and international organizations ends up in European banks and treasuries. Over the past decade alone, Palestinian leaders have received enough money to settle all Palestinian refugees on the Cote d'Azur.

These facts being matters of public knowledge, one wonders when liberals will finally ask for some answers from Palestinian leaders. Or is the criticism of Israel just an avenue for liberals to express rabid anti-Semitism?

CHAPTER TWO: The International Press and Israel

The spurious claims of a supposed Jewish stranglehold over the western press have been repeated so often that they have become conventional wisdom to many uninformed people around the world. The Arab and Iranian media would like the world to believe that the alleged Jewish control has produced slanted coverage of the Middle East crisis favorable to Israel.

For those who bother to follow the coverage of the region by western news media, the evidence is overwhelming that Israel is the victim of bias and press malpractice. Other than North Korea, no country or government in the world has been as vilified in the western media as Irael.

You will seldom see a positive story about the state of Israel in the European and North American press. Israeli achievements, its contributions to efforts at saving lives, including those of people in Islamic countries, are either under-reported or totally ignored.

Coverage of Israeli politics is almost exclusively centered on the role of clownish extremist minority parties, with little mention made of the vibrancy of the only functioning democracy in the region, in spite of constant aggression from the dictatorships that surround it. Perhaps the American press is too embarrassed to admit that the Israeli democracy is so representative that Arabs and more recent immigrants from Ethiopia have better representation in the Knesset than African-Americans have in the US Senate.

The same western media finds it very difficult to acknowledge Israeli benevolence on the international scene. During the Haitian crisis in 2010, all media attention was focused on generous fund-raising in the west. But the most effective and efficient assistance Haitians received after the floods came from a quickly-established Israeli medical facility that saved thousands of lives. The supposedly pro-Israel western press totally ignored this contribution or mentioned it as an afterthought.

The same can be said of Israeli development aid to Africa. Most of the sub-Saharan states that have attained self-sufficiency in food production are beneficiaries of Israeli agricultural expertise. Each dollar of Israeli assistance to Africa produces more benefits to the local population than ten thousand dollars of World Bank-funded projects and western development aid.

The worst anti-Israel press coverage in the west actually comes from the American media, especially that part actually under Jewish control viz the New York Times Group. A review of the New York *Times* over the past decade failed to produce one report favorable to Israel by its reporters or editorial writers.

However, the crown for anti-Israel reporting in America has to be awarded to CNN and its Anderson Cooper. Their anti-Israel bias has become so pernicious that many Israelis now consider Al Jazeera a more reliable source of information about the Middle Eastern region. Anderson Cooper's performance during the 2012 Pillar of Defense operation was the quintessential example of bias and shoddy reporting—a disgrace to journalism.

Cooper and CNN joined other western press organizations in accusing Israel of deliberately targeting an international press building in Gaza. What he glossed over, but was essential to the story, was that the supposed 'press building' was also a Hamas intelligence communications center. The media organizations that took residence in the building knew or should have known that their neighbors were terrorists and therefore legitimate military targets.

Anderson Cooper repeatedly made reference to the high Palestinian casualties in comparison to less than half a dozen Israeli losses. At the same time, he made light of the fact that Hamas fired some 1500 rockets into Israel almost exclusively aimed at civilian targets and population centers. One of these rockets actually hit a high school in Askalon and could have caused hundreds of casualties had the school been in session.

Anderson Cooper was in Gaza when the international press broadcast pictures of dead children from the Syrian war as though they were victims of Israeli bombing. He was here when the picture of a supposedly dead child was broadcast, only to have the child be caught running down the next block a few minutes later. In both cases, the CNN correspondent made no effort to condemn the misinformation.

Cooper reported the lynching of five young Gazans accused of spying for Israel. CNN failed to tell the world that the victims were Christian. Cooper made no effort to verify the accuracy of the accusations against the victims, even when their families did everything possible to challenge the reports.

The young men had been killed because they were Christian and some of their relatives had been critical of Hamas leaders for provoking Israel and inviting the attack on Gaza.

Much of Cooper's coverage of the 2012 crisis was centered on the devastation caused by Israeli air strikes, hence the regular updates of Palestinian casualties. The obvious implication of his reporting was to portray the meanness and brutality of the Israeli armed forces. In the same vein, he had to withhold any information that would seem to provide a rational explanation of Israeli operations. Firstly, most of the Palestinian casualties were the result of Hamas embedding military targets among heavily populated civilian institutions. This is a war crime per the Geneva Convention. It is well known that all the terrorist organizations in the region tend to hide their weapons in schools, mosques, and civilian-occupied buildings. If Cooper was unaware of this, he has no business pretending to be a knowledgeable reporter in the region.

Secondly, many of the deaths in Gaza resulted from secondary explosions from Hamas munition dumps that had been hit and which happened to be in or near civilian-occupied buildings.

Finally, many Gazans were killed be either mishandled or misfired Hamas rockets.

There was obvious colluding between the reporters in Gaza to avoid any mention, much less praise, of the diligence and precision with which the Israeli forces operated. No other air force in the world besides Israel could have left so little collateral damage after so many bombing runs. Compared to the NATO bombings in Afghanistan, Israeli pilots during the Pillar of Defense were absolute aces.

The western media claim to have veteran knowledgeable reporters in the region. Some, like CNN, even have resident correspondents in Israel. Anderson Cooper has been to the region on numerous occasions. It is surprising that he has never met a Palestinian who is critical of Hamas or the Palestinian Authority. If he has, he has never shared their views with his audiences.

The interviews of Palestinians we have seen from Cooper are done in the public square with Hamas minders watching on to make sure the interviewee sticks to the party line. Everyone including Cooper knows what would happen to them and their families if they uttered the mildest criticism of their leaders. Yet he lends his microphone, his reputation, and that of his organization to the charade time and time again. In spite of his numerous visits to the region,

Cooper is still unaware that 65% of Arab business owners in East Jerusalem are opposed to being put under the rule of the Palestinian Authority and have pledged to move if that ever happens. Cooper also does not know that Palestinian investors put six times more investments in Israel than in Palestinian territory. Finally, he also does not know that Arab Israelis and Palestinians living in Israel have twenty times the chance of attending college than those under the Palestinian Authority's rule.

If Cooper and his friends of the western media know these facts, they are not sharing them with their audiences. Perhaps because such revelations may go against the demonic image of Israel they would like to leave with their audiences.

Israelis and supporters of Israel are often baffled at the shoddiness and anti-partisanship of reporting on the Middle East by CNN and much of the European media. For some, Anderson Cooper is just a mild manifestation of the centuries-old anti-Semitism of the white Anglo-Saxon Protestant. For others, it is just the product of lazy reporters unable or unwilling to put in the efforts that fair-minded investigative reporting requires.

There may be another explanation for the shoddy work of western reporters concerning the Israeli-Palestinian conflict. Western reporters are aware that, as a functioning democracy since its creation, Israel has made strenuous efforts to guarantee freedom of the press, even during wartime. It has striven to give maximum protection to journalists irrespective of their ideological leanings.

Hamas, Fatah, the PLO, and PA, like all other repressive regimes of the region, have no tolerance for a critical press. Their supporters and operatives will not hesitate to kidnap, torture, and kill reporters that are critical of their leaders or organizations.

So, while Anderson Cooper is welcomed and protected in Israel notwithstanding his anti-Israel bias, one faux pas with the Palestinians would have a fatwa hanging around his neck. While protecting its proud tradition of press freedoms, Israel will have to develop new strategies to fight the damaging effects of dangerous reporters like Cooper.

CHAPTER THREE: The Failures of Israeli Diplomacy

Just as the state of Israel has been extremely proficient in military, intelligence, and economic matters, successive Israeli governments have been extremely deficient in the area of public diplomacy. The admission of the Palestinian Authority to UNESCO and its more recent success at the United Nations General Assembly can in part be credited to the sloppiness and failures of Israeli diplomacy.

In Africa, at least 30 states are predisposed to be allies and friends of Israel. In Central and South America, Israel should be able to find another 15 dependable allies.

The majority of black African states have majority Christian populations with a particularly strong attachment to the Holy Land. Unfortunately, Israeli diplomats in most of these countries appear to be working from bunkers. They seem to believe that their assignment is limited to working with government and seldom develop relationships with civil society and local Christian leaders.

Many local journalists, including those favorably inclined to Israel, have great difficulties having appointments with Israeli diplomats. It takes two weeks for a senior reporter or editor to arrange for an interview or a mere sit-down with a senior diplomat at the Israeli embassy.

Israeli diplomats in Africa do not believe that their duties include explaining their policy positions to the local populations of their host country, to elicit their support and potentially have them lobby their leadership on behalf of Israel. Had there been such local pro-Israel pressure groups, the five African Foreign Ministers who received bribes for the votes of their delegations at UNESCO and at the UN for the Palestinian Authority would have at the worst hesitated, and at best, rejected those overtures. It was easier for them to accept the bribes because they knew nobody in the home countries cared much about the Middle Eastern crisis.

In Africa, no government seems to be more inept at self-promotion than the Israeli government. When France, Britain, or the United States spends a dollar in Africa, there is a real carnival and fanfare with the mobilization of the local press and flag-flying ceremonies. Whereas, Israel undertakes the most successful development projects in Africa and nobody hears about them. You have to go to some obscure websites to learn about the highly successful agricultural projects and rural solar energy projects undertaken by Israeli organizations in Africa.

The spread of Islamic fundamentalism in the Sahel region should open new vistas and opportunities for Israel, even in those countries with large Muslim populations. Fundamentalism is alien to the Islam practiced in black Africa and most people in the region do not take kindly to the export of this threat to their religion by forces allied to or friendly with Hamas and Hezbollah.

Rather than take advantage of this situation, Israel chooses to outsource its courtship of Africa to the United States under the mistaken belief that the administration of an African-American president would have more gravitas with African leaders.

Unfortunately for Israel, the Obama administration has the lowest support in Africa since the Nixon presidency. Even the Bush administration won more respect and was considered more responsive to African interests than the present US government.

President Obama started off on the wrong foot with Africa by appointing Susan Rice as ambassador to the United Nations. The African delegation remembered Rice for her role in misleading President Clinton during the Rwandan crisis and in preventing Europe and the UN from intervening early to stop the genocide.

She made matters worse by misleading the Obama administration into blindly following the French into the Ivoirian conflict against the advice of America's closest allies on the continent. In the Libyan conflict, actions by the US diminished the efforts of the African Union, angering both Nigeria and South Africa, the most powerful nations south of the Sahara. When African governments started warning about loose Libyan weapons flowing across the continent, Rice did not take them seriously. Not only have these weapons turned up in the Sudan, they have also been used in the destabilization of the Central African Republic and more recently, Mali and Algeria.

Unlike previous administrations that started specific initiatives for Africa, this administration has nothing to show in Africa for its first four years. It is no surprise that Susan Rice is the most despised UN ambassador by the African delegation since the Kissinger era. It is thus not surprising that President Obama could not even get his Kenyan cousins to support Israel at the UN or at UNESCO.

If Israel hopes to reverse its recent diplomatic failures, it needs to put its diplomats to work in Africa and in Central and South America. On both these continents, they go into battle with a lot of potential friends and allies.

Africa's largest Christian population and the increasing threats from Islamic fundamentalism are advantages that Israeli diplomacy can harness. Another advantage for Israel is the increasing alienation of African nations from their former colonial masters. Contrary to the blind allegiance of African leaders of the past decades to their former masters, the new leaders are now in search of new allies and partners in their development efforts. Israel happens to have more to offer Africa in such areas as agriculture, managing water resources, and the development of alternative renewable energy sources than Europe and America.

In order to succeed, the government of Israel at a minimum will need to do three things. The first would be to develop more government to government relations, requiring more Israeli embassies in Africa. Second, Israel and pro-Israel organizations should engage local civil society in their efforts to build relations. Finally, there should be a very serious and sustained effort to mobilize Christian organizations as advocates for the state of Israel.

This should not be too difficult because African Christian leaders have always felt a kinship with, and a commitment to, the land of their savior. Now they are anxious for Israeli advice on how to protect their flock and churches from rampaging jihadists.

For Jews, Israel, and Israel's friends, it is time to abandon false modesty and to celebrate the contributions of Jews and Judaism to human civilization. They gave the world monotheism. Judaism begot Christianity and Islam. 50% of the Koran is lifted from the Torah and another 25% from the New Testament. Without Judaism, there would not have been Mohammedanism.

Beyond religion, we also need to celebrate the tremendous contributions of Jews to all aspects of human knowledge and our way of life today. We know that the father of modern sociology Emile Durkheim was a Jew but many other Jews in music, literature, and philosophy have shaped the intellectual evolution of human society for thousands of years.

Since the Nobel Prize was instituted, more than 40 Jewish scientists have awarded that prize: 12 in physics, 5 in chemistry, and 18 in medicine. Paul Ehlick, who discovered the treatment for syphilis, was Jewish. Israeli scientists developed Laquinimod and Copaxone for the treatment of multiple sclerosis. Rasagiline, which treats Parkinson's disease, was developed in Israel as well. These are just a few of the many therapies the world owes to Jews.

The state of Israel is second in the world in computer engineering and space science. It is fifth in clean technologies. Israel invented drip irrigation technology that has helped increase food production around the world and saved millions from hunger. Never have so many owed so much to so few. These achievements should be celebrated so that we can shame those who hate Jews, most of whom owe their very lives to the victims of their hate. Most of the decrepit leaders of Iran and the equally so Arab sheiks and monarchs who sponsor anti-Semitic terrorism would not be alive but for the drugs and medical devices produced by Jewish ingenuity.

Let us challenge the Middle Eastern Jew haters who rob their nations only to go gamble away that wealth at Jewish-owned casinos from Monaco to Las Vegas to Macao. And those others whose massive fortunes are entrusted to Jewish lawyers and bankers.

Let us celebrate a people and a nation that, against all odds, have continued to strive to make the world a better place for all. This is not just the duty of the government and people of Israel, it is the duty of all honest people who have benefitted from the labors of a people we have betrayed over and over again.

CHAPTER FOUR: The Failures of the Israel Lobby in America

The contributions of American Jews and the Israel lobby in America to the early survival and development of the state of Israel can never be overemphasized.

American Jews not only financed and sustained emigration to Israel, they also provided vital financial sustenance for the nascent Jewish state. Furthermore, their effective lobbying in Washington insured American financial and military aid to the young state.

For all this and more, the people of Israel will be eternally grateful to their American brethren for their solidarity.

However, for the past decade, the Israel lobby in Washington has increasingly become more of a liability than an asset to Israel. This lobby has, as we will show, failed to evolve with the times, in terms of Israel's changing needs. Many in the community have transformed advocacy for Israel into a means of personal political advancement. They have also failed to recognize the changing politic realities of American politics.

For over two decades, support of Israel has become the most lucrative racket in America. Various lobbying groups and American politicians are more concerned about the benefits that devolve to them for their advocacy for Israel than the real benefits to Israel itself.

American politicians and so-called pro-Israel lobbying organizations have strived to portray support of Israel as a favor to the Jewish state and as an extra burden to the American taxpayer. This is the primary postulation that enabled them to raise large sums of money from an unsuspecting Jewish American community that is very supportive of Israel.

In reality, Israel is not the dependent step-child that it is painted as. The real story of the Israeli-American relationship indeed reveals the United States as the principal financial beneficiary. American taxpayer investments in support of the Jewish state are in fact the most lucrative investments made on their behalf in the last half century.

It is true that the United States of America was one of the 33 nations that voted in favor of Resolution 181 on November 29, 1947 at the United Nations calling for the establishment of a Jewish state and an Arab state in Palestine. Thereafter, the US government did little or nothing to insure the survival of the young state of Israel when it was proclaimed in 1948.

The US did nothing to persuade Great Britain, the mandatory Power of Palestine, to live up to the stipulations of Resolution 181 which, among other things, required that it supervise the creation of a provisionary authority referred to as Commission that would transition into the two-state solution.

The United States did nothing to prevent Britain from handing over its weaponry to Arab terrorist organizations that were making open preparations for the destruction of the new Jewish state. And it did nothing to protect the young state from invading armies of the Arab League, when that organization openly defied the United Nations and declared war on Israel in 1948.

The first substantive American intervention in the region was not in Palestine but rather in Iran where, in 1953, at the behest of the Standard Oil Company and British Petroleum, the US overthrew the democratically elected and legitimate government of Iranian Prime Minister Dr. Mohammad Mossadegh. They replaced him with the corrupt and brutal dictatorship of Mohammed Reza Pahlavi, the last "Shah of Iran," which paved the way for the present and even more brutal dictatorship of the Ayatollahs.

Its next intervention in the Middle East was in 1956 during the Suez Canal crisis that putted the Egyptians against the French and the British. This intervention was not in support of Israel but rather, in support of NATO allies. Although the Suez Canal crisis derived from the desire of then Egyptian President Gamal Abdel Nasser's to assert Egyptian sovereignty against the neo-colonialist behavior of his European partners, American saw it as an attempt by the Soviet Union to strike at the Western Alliance through an Arab surrogate.

Although born under difficult circumstances in a land with very limited resources, through the resourcefulness of its people and strong support in the wake of the Jewish diaspora, Israel developed rapidly both economically and militarily and by 1970, was a force to be reckoned with on the world scene. At that point, it had become the lynchpin of American Middle East policy and not the weak link.

The importance of Israel to the US did not evolve by happenstance. It started with the 1969 overthrow of King Isris I of Libya by Muammar Qaddafi. With massive oil wealth, the new Libyan leader was intent on joining forces with Nasser of Egypt, Assad of Syria, and the Ba'ath party of Iraq in ridding the Middle East of the last vestiges of western imperialism by overthrowing all of the monarchies.

The plan was to start with the elimination of the Hashemite Monarchy of Jordan, which would then be handed over to the radical leader of Fatah. This job was assigned to Syria. Iraq was assigned the task of overthrowing the Kuwait monarchy, which was to be followed by a pan-Arab assault on Saudi Arabia and the other Gulf monarchies.

The execution of this grand realignment of the Middle East started in September 1970, when Syria engineered a Palestinian revolt in Jordan. This was intended to soften up the Jordanian regime just before the Syrian Army would move in under the pretext of protecting the Palestinian populations from massacre.

Just as Syrian President Hafez al-Assad mobilized the Syrian Army to move into Jordan, King Hussein appealed to Israel for assistance. The Israelis warned Assad that any movement of his troops would be met by a determined response. Assad "chickened out" and left the Palestinians to be slaughtered by the Jordanian forces.

The Syrian-Palestinian misadventure in Jordan had a profound effect on the realignment of the players on the Middle Eastern political chessboard.

Firstly, the failure resulted in serious dissension and distrust among the radicals. Syria blamed Egypt for failing to come to its assistance by not opening a western front against Israel to divert its attention from the Jordanian front. Libya suspected Egypt of playing a double game and stopped its subsidies to Egypt.

Secondly, prior to the founding of the terrorist Black September Organization (BSO) in 1970, the Arab monarchies had been looking for ways to accommodate the Soviet bloc which was the backbone of the radical states. They thought they could insulate themselves from the Cold War by throwing a few lucrative military (and other) contracts to the Soviet Union, thereby loosening their ties to the radicals.

After the BSO fiasco, the Gulf monarchies decided to throw their lot entirely with the western alliance. All defense contracts worth billions of dollars were annually awarded to the United States, Britain, and France. They also proceeded to improve the collaboration between their intelligence agencies with Israel, which had now become a credible guarantor of their survival.

Western oil companies were given carte blanche in the region, and the west was guaranteed reasonable control over both the supply and cost of oil. Since then, these oil companies have legally and illegally taken out trillions of dollars from the region.

The monarchies went even further in tying the fate of their kingdoms to that of Western economies. They started hoarding western government debt in the form of treasury bonds, thereby keeping down the cost of borrowing for American and European taxpayers and subsidizing government spending.

Today, Saudi Arabia holds over $600 billion in US Treasury bonds and other Gulf kingdoms collectively hold another $400 billion in US public debt.

Considering the destruction the Ayatollahs in Tehran willingly wrought upon the Iranian economy, can you imagine what they would be willing to visit on the world economy if they could lay their hands on more than a trillion dollars of US Treasury bonds?

Since 1970, Israel has been the principal guarantor of the survival of the monarchies that have provided all the above windfalls for the west, particularly the United States. Without Israel, the

US would have had to do this all on its own. We saw what it cost in terms of American treasure and American lives to wrestle the Kuwaiti monarachy from the claws of Saddam Hussein. The second Iraq War has cost an estimated $823 billion (according to Bloomberg.com) and the lives of more than 4,000 American servicemen.

The United States has over 50,000 deployed military personnel stationed in Japan and nearly 30,000 deployed in South Korea. To secure the Arab monarchies, in the absence of Israel, the United States would have had to station at least 100,000 troops in the region. The annual cost of one American soldier deployed to Iraq in 2011 is estimated to be a staggering $685,000 per year according to numbers from the Washington-based Center for Strategic and Budgetary Assessments' *Analysis of the FY2011 Defense Budget.*

American institutional supporters of Israel, in various politicians and Jewish organizations, have sought to present Israel as a ward to the United States and misrepresent to the world that US aid to the Jewish state is dependent on their work.

Nothing is further from the truth. These groups and individuals are more interested in enhancing their self-importance and fleecing unsuspecting Jewish Americans than defending the true interests of Israel.

The truth about the Israel-American relationship is that the Jewish state is being fleeced by its American partner. Whatever aid the US gives Israel is minuscule in comparison to the benefits America derives from the Israeli presence in the Middle East.

The most powerful and effective lobbyists for Israel in America are American oil companies, the military-industrial complex, the US Treasury Department, and the Arab monarchies of the Gulf region.

It is not by accident that the only major news organization that has been a relentless supporter of Israel in America is Fox News Corporation, through its television and newspaper holdings. The largest shareholder, next to the Murdochs, is Saudi Prince Alwaleed bin Talal.

In the 1970's, the Soviet Union was bent on promoting open warfare between Israel and the Arab states. They saw in a Middle Eastern war, an opportunity to sell arms to the rich oil-producing states of Libya and Iraq that were willing to pay for the poorer states of Syria and Egypt. The Soviets also viewed a Middle Eastern war as a means of disrupting and even destroying the economies of the west that were so dependent on Middle Eastern oil.

To that end, the Soviet government presented intercepted Nixon anti-Semitic rantings to Egyptian, Syrian, and Iraqi political and military leaders in an attempt to convince the Arabs that President Nixon would be the least likely of American leaders to come to the aid of Israel in the event of a war.

The late Egyptian President Anwar Sadat decided to confirm Nixon's feelings about Israel, and on several occasions during meetings with him, threatened imminent war with Israel and wondered what America would do.

On one occasion, after trying unsuccessfully to calm the bellicose Sadat, Nixon turned and looked straight at him and said: "Whatever you do, let me assure you that if Israel is attacked, American will intervene fully and strongly in her support. American support for Israel is unconditional notwithstanding whatever personal feelings I might have about Jews or about the state of Israel."

The message Sadat received, and which he dutifully relayed to his Arab colleagues, was that American interests in the region that were protected by Israel trumped the personal prejudices of any American leader.

For American politicians and various Jewish lobbying groups in Washington, D.C., support for Israel is a business; some would say a "racket." They are in it firstly for the money they can make and secondarily for their own self-aggrandizement. Defending Israeli interests is only incidental.

In the process, many of them have become more of an albatross around the neck of those who are genuinely interested in promoting the cause of Israel in America. Leading American politicians prostituting their alleged support has become rampant.

Joseph Liebermann, former senator from Connecticut, for all but the last several years of his political career was a loyal democrat and credible advocate for Israel. Liebermann was so comfortable with the Democratic Party's Israeli policy that he even had words of praise for President Jimmy Carter's Middle Eastern policy. He was so comfortable with the party's platform that he even ran on their national ticket for the post of Vice President in 2004.

A few years ago, the Connecticut electorate at the Democratic primary election rejected him and he became an independent. To raise money and earn some votes, "Support for Israel" became his only slogan. Suddenly, all his former colleagues in the Democratic Party were now presented as "weak-kneed" about Israel and went all out to support US President George W. Bush's adventurism in the Middle East, which turned out to be seriously detrimental to the interests of Israel.

Notwithstanding the testimony of the most prominent Israeli military, intelligence, and political leaders about the high level of support Israel had received from the Obama administration, Liebermann went after President Obama with a vengeance. In the process, he won nothing for Israel but rather, seriously damaged support for Israel among millions of Obama supporters. His only achievement was attracting a lot of money for his political action committee/campaign fund.

Another political hack using Israel for personal gain is Arizona Republican Senator John McCain. Though a persistent supporter of Israel, McCain's commitment to Israeli security grew leaps and bounds when he decided to run for the American Presidency in 2008. Suddenly, he could not seem to utter two sentences without mentioning the word "Israel." Again, he supported the second Iraq War without any consideration of the negative impact that would have on Israeli security, a different course from previous US presidential administrations. He succeeded in leeching millions of dollars from the Jewish-American community.

Then came Mitt Romney, whose political philosophy and policy positions changed from one day to another. He presented himself as the God-sent protector of Israel and harped on the close relationship he had with Prime Minister Netanyahu…a relationship that was nothing but a figment of Romney's imagination. The former presidential candidate was a man who cared so much about Israel that his first visit to the country was to raise funds, successfully conning the Jewish-American community out of well over $100 million.

Another political figure is about to join the gang. Florida Republican Senator Marco Rubio is making his first visit to Israel just as he is being mentioned as a candidate for the 2016 Presidential Sweepstakes.

Senator Rubio, a self-described devout Christian, has never considered a pilgrimage to Israel, either to visit the holy sites or show solidarity with the people of Israel during its most trying of moments. But now his ambitions toward higher political office are taking him to Israel with the belief that it will help among Jewish-American "suckers" ready to be separated from their money. Lest we forget, Senator Rubio is an unapologetic member and supporter of the Tea Party, whose policies of isolationism have best been enunciated by the father-son combination of Ron and Rand Paul.

One of the biggest threats to Israel-American relations is in fact the Tea Party, which is really an amalgamation of the isolationist extreme right wing of American politics and white supremacist groups, many of them sponsored by the billionaire Koch brothers. Using the classic fascist tactic of disinformation by claiming an imaginary Obama "hatred" for Israel, the Tea Party has been attracting increasing numbers of otherwise intelligent and sane Jewish-Americans, mostly in Florida, the other southern states, and mid-Western states. This reeks eerily of the Weimar Republic in 1920's Germany, an era many American Jews are uncomfortable talking about.

Those were the early years of the Nationalist Socialist Party, when a destitute Adolf Hitler was struggling to form his party. Hitler trumpeted his hatred for Communists, trade unions, and homosexuals—people he classified as traitors of the Fatherland that had to be crushed like cockroaches. German Jewish businesses rushed to give Hitler their money and thus fertilized the seed that grew into their destruction.

The hate of the closet racist wing of the Tea Party is today primarily directed at blacks, Hispanics, and Asians. These people have also accused President Obama of having handed over "their" White House to the Jews. They are the same individuals who blamed the near economic collapse of 2008 not on the stupidity of the [2001-2009] Bush presidency but rather, on the so-called "greedy Jewish bankers" who control Wall Street.

History has a canny way of repeating itself and political mistakes invariably produce the same results. A perceived alliance between Jewish-Americans and the Tea Party is inimical to the interests of Israel, even in the short-term, and alienates the large parts of the American population that are the present recipients of the attacks and insults of closet racists. These vilified minorities of today will become the majority in the not-so-distant future.

The position espoused here is that over the past four decades, the so-called Israeli lobby in America has been, for the most part, a combination of political hacks and swindlers ripping off unsuspecting American Jewry who are deeply and earnestly committed to the safety, survival, and progress of Israel.

These charlatans and hucksters have successfully fooled the world and most Americans that the US has continually made sacrifices for Israel. The truth is that Israel has earned every penny America has sent its way and worse, that the benefits of that aid have mostly accrued to the United States. For reasons explained earlier in this chapter, Israel did not need AIPAC, Liebermann, or McCain to get the pittance it received from the United States.

However, more than ever before, Israel will need an effective lobbying operation in American in the years to come. This lobbying will not be one geared towards throwing money at politicians but rather, one geared towards co-opting the people of America to the cause of a Jewish state of Israel.

The necessity of a new approach is due to two major impending changes in America: the development of new sources of energy for American and world markets, as well as the changing cultural, political, and economic demographics of the United States, including the ongoing and growing empowerment of women.

More than ever before, the United States is today committed to energy independence. The continuing development of alternative energy sources such as solar, wind, nuclear, hydro, and biomass conversion, and an increased drilling for fossil fuels, including the controversial use of fracking, coal liquefaction, and oil extraction from tundra, will make the United States energy independent within the next two decades. Conservative estimates see America not only energy independent but also a net exporter of energy within that span of time.

Furthermore, greater exploration and drilling in Latin America, Africa, and in the South China Sea is set to increase oil production to the extent that the Gulf region will cease to be a major player, and supplier, on the world oil markets. With the world economy liberated from the capricious tyranny of Middle Eastern dictators, the region will cease to be an area of strategic importance to the United States and its Western allies.

On the internal front, there are major political developments coming with the aforementioned changing demographics of the US population and which will no doubt impact Israel-American relations.

To begin with, by 2030, the white Aryan population will become a minority in America as a combination of the so-called "People of Color," i.e., blacks, Hispanics, and Asians, become the (collective) majority. This new majority will also become the source of the majority of the Armed Forces of the United States and will, no doubt, want political power to match their added contribution to the life of the nation.

More importantly, the changing demographics are also setting in a change of the guard in the political leadership in those communities. The new black and Hispanic leaders are not wedded to the alliances of the past. Most of them were not even born during the historic mid-twentieth century and ongoing civil rights struggles that saw black and Hispanic leaders join forces with Jewish advocates and activists. Today, most people in the black and Hispanic communities view the Jewish community as part of the white power structure that has exploited them and sought to keep them down.

Finally, the traditional methods of campaigning that has facilitated the purchasing of politicians is being slowly replaced, as evidenced by the ineffectiveness of the billionaire Koch brothers, Sheldon Adelson, and "Wall Street moguls" in affecting the results of the 2012 presidential and congressional elections.

The introduction by the Obama campaign of a campaign driven by contributions "as little as ten dollars" has empowered the masses earlier bereft of influential means to gain a political toehold towards policy influence against the self-interests of millionaires and billionaires whose well-financed political action committees (PACs) and lobbyists are able to hold candidates for elective office captive. This has also encouraged the non-white communities to begin a build-up of indigenous political action funds that will liberate their candidates from their dependence on, and the tyranny of, outside political contributors.

Friends and supporters of Israel should no more depend on their ability to bribe a McCain, Rubio, or Romney. They will need to devise new strategies to promote the interests of Israel and to win the support of the various communities for the cause of Israel. For reasons too many to enumerate, this can be achieved at less expense than presently being unnecessarily wasted on sleazy politicians. The cause of Israel is not merely a just one; it is a compelling story when properly presented.

This is an area in which the friends of Israel and so-called "Jewish Lobby" have failed woefully. Obviously, it has been easier to just throw money away at politicians and organizing parties. Now the real work needs to begin.

Before we get to the real work of advocacy, those who would support the Israeli cause in America should be ready to put all their efforts in this country. Though the people of Israel have always appreciated the help of Jewish-Americans, they have rightly been appalled by those American supporters who constantly seek to interfere with Israeli politics.

There are some Jewish-Americans and organizations who think that their financial contribution to Israel gives them the right to criticize Israeli leaders. In fact, by criticizing Israeli leaders abroad, these friends of Israel give comfort to the enemies of Israel. Supporters of Israel who are uncomfortable with an Israeli leader should be able to make such representations in private. But should they feel even more strongly, they are at liberty to immigrate to Israel and directly participate in the political process.

That said, the enormous task of advocating for Israel in the new America is so daunting that, if done properly, American friends of Israel will have little time and energy to concern themselves with how the people of Israel manage their democracy.

Of all developed countries, Americans appear to be the most uniformed in history and world affairs. Until September 11, 2001, when Al Qaeda brought its religious fanaticism to the United

States, Americans were generally insulated from major international events. A very poor liberal arts educational system, materialism, and an immersion in sitcoms and professional sports have all led to Americans being generally more detached from major world events since the conclusion of World War II.

That is why American political leaders have been able, on behalf of private corporations, to engage in egregious criminal behavior around the world, making enemies all along the way. That is why most Americans who are very generous and good people cannot understand the level of anti-Americanism around the world.

That is why, even though most Americans are favorably predisposed towards Israel, most of them are very ignorant about the story of Israel. Most Americans believe that Jews are an alien population in the Middle East and are mostly immigrants grabbing on to ancestral Arab lands. Most Americans also believe that Israel has been responsible for most, if not all, of the Palestinian population now in their own diaspora and in refugee camps through the Middle East.

Friends of Israel should be advocating for inclusion of the history of Palestine in American high schools and colleges. Not just the history from 1945 but rather, from 5,000 years ago. The study of comparative religions will reveal that the Middle East was Judaic long before Christianity and Islam. This goes to the question of legitimacy of the Judaic claims to the Holy Land.

The history of Palestine since 1948 shows that Palestinians were asked and encouraged to leave Palestine by the Arab League so that advancing Arab armies would not be impeded in clearing the region of Jews, to facilitate their eventual return. Others voluntarily sold their lands to finance immigration to other parts of the region and the world. More Palestinians were pushed into exile out of Palestine by the Kingdom of Jordan after their 1970 war than by Israel since 1948.

Finally, and most importantly, Americans should be told why they should be personally invested in the survival and well-being of Israel. Israel is the only state in the Middle East where Christians can freely worship. In Egypt, where the Coptics have lived for more than 2,000 years, their churches are being burned. In the other Arab states, the mere possession of a bible can mean death. With the desecration of religious sites all over the world by Islamic fundamentalists, a Jewish state of Israel is the only guarantor of the safeguard and survival of holy Christian sites in the Holy Land.

The legitimacy of a Jewish state of Israel should not be difficult to establish within the present minority (future majority) communities in the United States. There is already enough goodwill in the black and Hispanic communities because of the importance of the Christian church and the strength of their faith.

The Israeli lobby in America has so far not been very successful in having a meaningful presence in the black and Hispanic communities for many reasons. Their greatest impediment has been a know-all attitude that has prevented them from seeking the assistance they need. Everybody pretends to know minority communities better than the indigenous. Like all other population groups, there have been tremendous changes since the days of the earlier cited civil rights movements. These communities are far more eclectic today in terms of national origins and socio-cultural origins than they were 20 or 30 years ago.

Immigration from Africa and the Caribbean has brought significant changes to the black population of America. Puerto Ricans and Cubans are no more the principal or dominant groups in the Hispanic community.

Though a Dr. Alan Dershowitz may be a very knowledgeable and eloquent advocate for Israel at Harvard or Princeton, he will not have the credibility of a black pastor or black activist in Harlem or in a black neighborhood in Detroit. Jewish-American supporters of Israel should join forces with friends from various communities and make them the spokespeople for Israel in their communities. Friends of Israel groups should be created in the various communities and generate support for Israel in their respective neighborhoods. School exchange programs and holiday camps in Israel for black and Hispanic children would go a long way in developing childhood friendships that would last a long time and pay more dividends for Israel than the purchase or bribery of a few political leaders.